AF322684

The Savior is Born
A Nativity Story

The reason for the season:

The story of Christmas is very special because it reminds us of the day Jesus Christ, the Son of God, was born. A long time ago, God promised to send a Savior to help everyone, and that Savior was Jesus. He was born in a little town called Bethlehem, not in a fancy palace but in a simple stable, surrounded by love.

Christmas is important because it's the day we celebrate Jesus coming to the world to bring peace, hope, and love to everyone. When we hear about the angels, the shepherds, and the wise men, it helps us remember how much God loves us and how Jesus came to show us the way to live with kindness and care for others.

That's what makes Christmas such a wonderful and joyful time—it's not just about presents, but about celebrating God's greatest gift to us all.

Matthew 1:23
Behold, a virgin shall be with child, and shall bring forth a son, and they shall call his name Emmanuel, which being interpreted is, God with us.

In Nazareth, a quiet town,
A girl named Mary knelt down.
An angel came with wings of light,
And filled her heart with sudden fright.

"Fear not," he said, "for God has chosen,
A gift for you, the door is open.
You'll bear a Son, His name is Jesus,
He'll be the One who comes to free us."

Mary bowed her head in awe,
And whispered, "I will follow God's law."
She knew this child would change the earth,
And bring to all a holy birth.

Matthew 1:20
But while he thought on these things,
behold, the angel of the Lord appeared unto
him in a dream, saying, Joseph, thou son of
David, fear not to take unto thee Mary thy
wife: for that which is conceived in her is
of the Holy Ghost.

Joseph, too, received a sign,
In a dream from God divine.
"Do not fear to take her hand,
For what she bears is God's own plan."

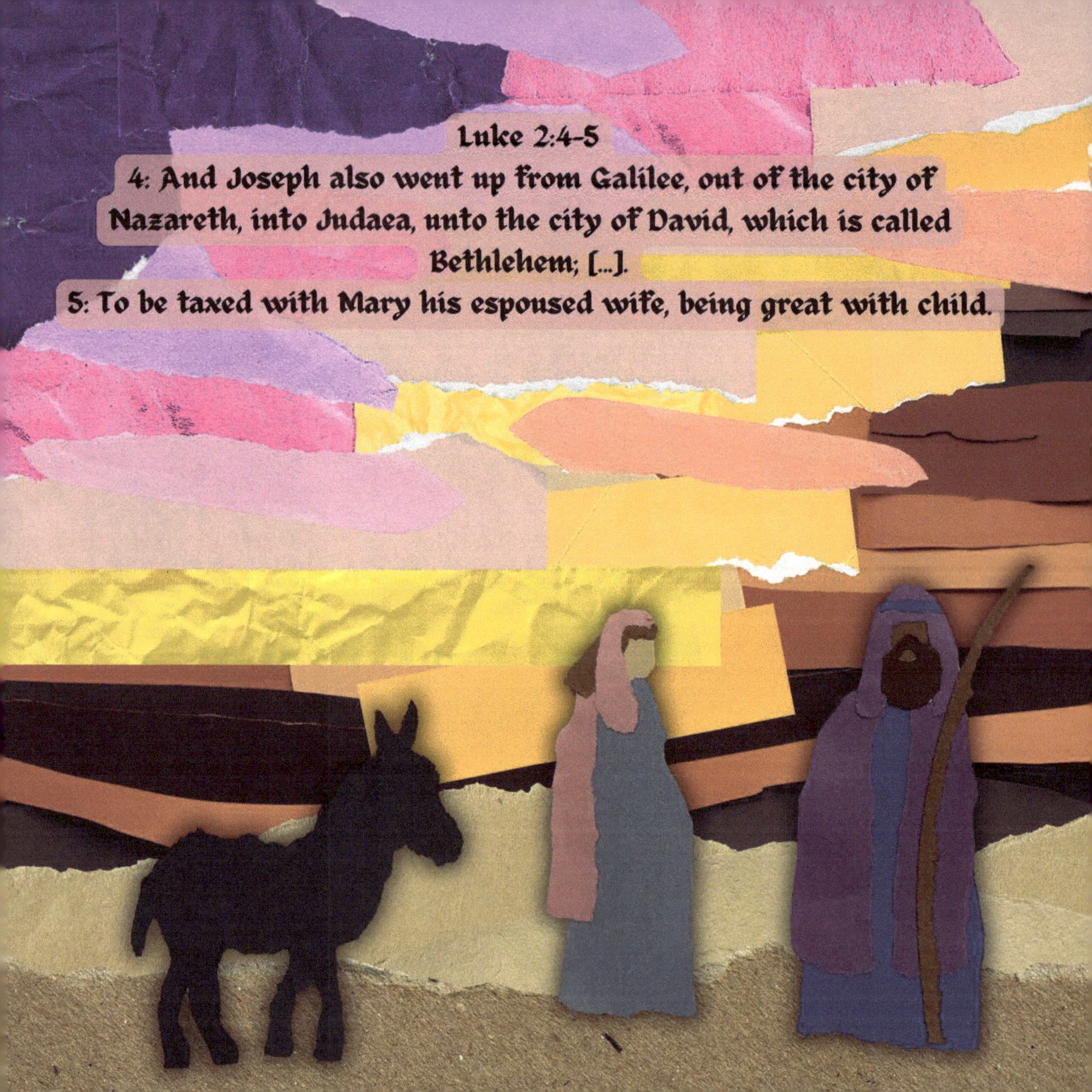

Luke 2:4-5
4: And Joseph also went up from Galilee, out of the city of Nazareth, into Judaea, unto the city of David, which is called Bethlehem; [...].
5: To be taxed with Mary his espoused wife, being great with child.

The road was long, the night was cold,
Through dusty paths and hills they strolled.
With weary steps, yet hearts held fast,
They journeyed on to Bethlehem at last.

Mary bore the weight and strain,
While Joseph led through wind and rain.
Each mile a test, each step a prayer,
Yet God's own purpose met them there.

Luke 2:7
And she brought forth her firstborn son, and wrapped him
in swaddling clothes, and laid him in a manger; because there
was no room for them in the inn.

In Bethlehem that quiet eve,
No place to stay, they had to leave.
The streets were full, the inns were tight,
No room for rest that weary night.

At last they found a humble stall,
A shelter low, with hay and straw.
Among the animals' gentle care,
They made their bed in the stable there.

And there, beneath the stars' soft glow,
In humble peace, with joy below,
The Savior of the world was born,
To bring the light of hope's new morn.

Luke 2:8-11
8: And there were in the same country shepherds abiding in the field, keeping watch over their flock by night.
9: And, lo, the angel of the Lord came upon them, and the glory of the Lord shone round about them: and they were sore afraid.
10: And the angel said unto them, Fear not: for, behold, I bring you good tidings of great joy, which shall be to all people.
11: For unto you is born this day in the city of David a Saviour, which is Christ the Lord.

The shepherds watched their flocks that night,
When the sky was filled with brilliant light.
An angel's voice rang clear and true,
"I bring good tidings to all of you."

In David's town, this wondrous day,
A Savior comes to lead the way.
You'll find Him wrapped in swaddling clothes,
With a mother's love He now grows."

Luke 2:13-14
13: And suddenly there was with the angel a multitude of the heavenly host praising God, and saying,
14: Glory to God in the highest, and on earth peace, good will toward men.

The heavens filled with songs of peace,
The shepherds' fear began to cease.
The angels spoke with voices clear,
"Rejoice, for God's salvation's near!

"Glory to God!" the angels sang,
As joyful praise through heaven rang.
On earth, let peace and goodwill shine,
For Christ is born, God's perfect sign.

The shepherds froze, their hearts amazed,
As heaven's light before them blazed.
They ran to see this wonder bright,
The Son of God, this holy light.

Luke 2:16
"And they came with haste, and found Mary, and Joseph, and the babe lying in a manger."

The shepherds came with hearts aflame,
Through fading stars and dawn's first flame.
With awe they gathered round to gaze,
At Christ, the Lord, in humble hay.

In the manger, soft and mild,
They found the holy, promised Child.
With wonder deep and joy to sing,
They praised the newborn, Heaven's King.

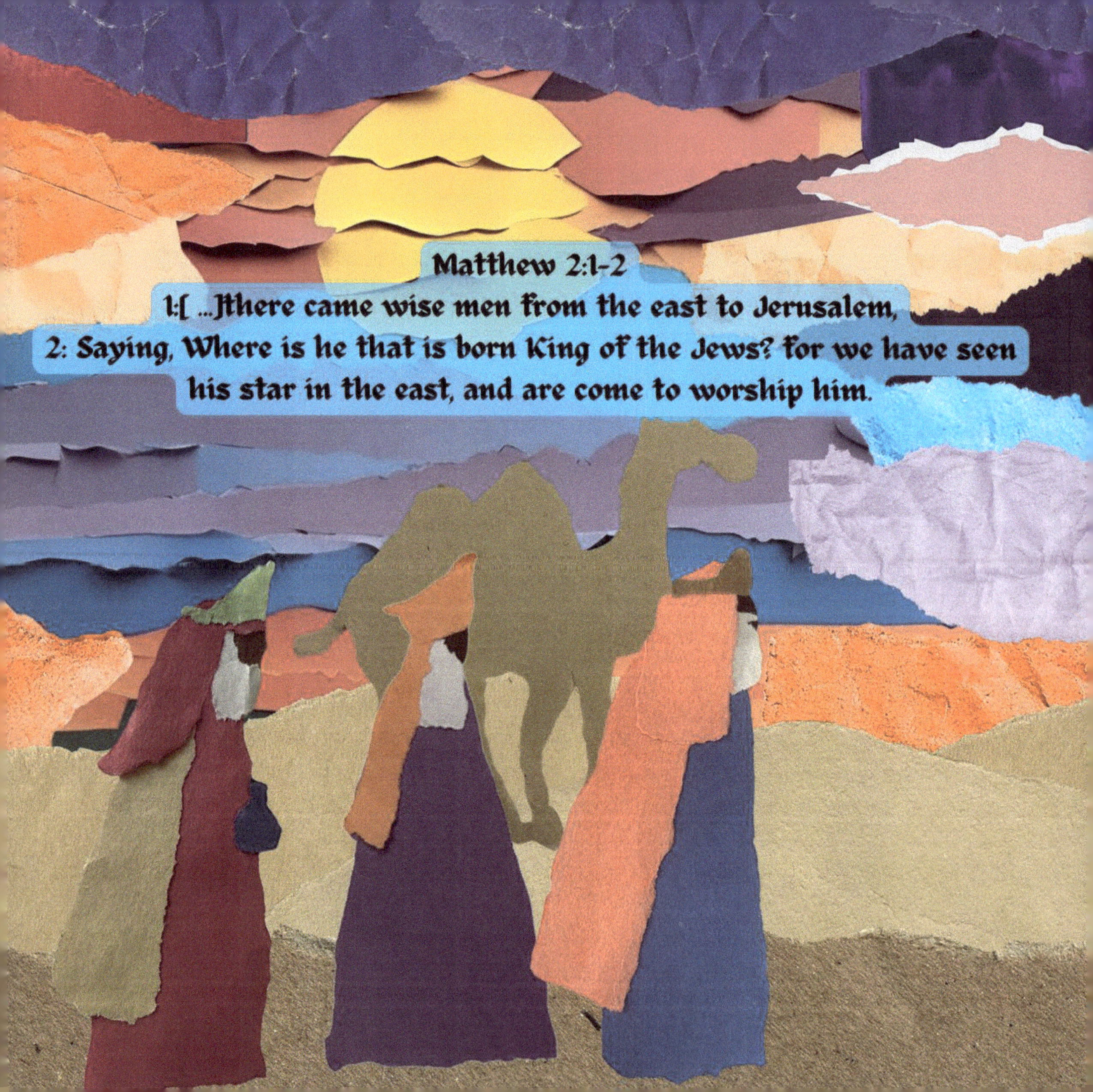

Matthew 2:1-2
1:[...]There came wise men from the east to Jerusalem,
2: Saying, Where is he that is born King of the Jews? for we have seen his star in the east, and are come to worship him.

From lands afar, wise men came,
They saw the star, they knew His name.
Through desert sands they made their way,
With gifts to honor Him that day.

Matthew 2:9-10
9: [...] and, lo, the star, [...] went before them, till it came and stood over where the young child was.
10: When they saw the star, they rejoiced with exceeding great joy.

For many days and weeks they came,
Through lands unknown, both rough and plain.
Months passed, the star relied upon,
With hope and faith, they pressed on.

Bearing treasures from lands afar,
They sought the Savior beneath the star.
It shone above, a light so true,
Guiding them close as nearer they drew.

Matthew 2:11
And when they were come into the house, they saw the young
child with Mary his mother, and fell down, and worshipped him:
and when they had opened their treasures, they presented unto
him gifts; gold, and frankincense, and myrrh.

Their journey's end, a light so bright,
The promised King within their sight.
They knelt in awe, with gifts in hand,
Rejoicing there in that holy land.

Gold, for a King so pure and true,
Frankincense, for prayers anew,
And myrrh, a gift for what would be,
A life of sacrifice to set us free.

And there He lay, in a bed of hay,
The Son of God on that first day.
A tiny child, so meek, so mild,
Yet in His face, all heaven smiled.

The Prince of Peace, the Lord of Light,
Was born to lead us through the night.
With love and grace, He'd pave the way,
And bring us hope on Christmas Day.

www.ingramcontent.com/pod-product-compliance
Lightning Source LLC
Chambersburg PA
CBHW040736150726
48196CB00011B/621